47 AMAZON FBA SECRETS OF A 7-FIGURE SELLER

Kevin Bosch

Table of Contents

Introduction

Imagine living the ultimate freedom lifestyle where you have complete control over your life and get to travel wherever you want, whenever you want!

Well apparently, as cliche as it may sound to some of you, this lifestyle has now become a reality for some folks out there and I am so excited to tell you that it could now become your reality too!

See, in the world we live in today, it has absolutely become possible for people like you and me to generate boatloads of cash right from our very fingertips. With simply just the use of a laptop and an internet connection, the search for that dream life you may be denying yourself all these years are now within a few clicks away!

And the biggest reason why I'm sharing this is because I am on a mission to spread awareness about the mind-blowing growth of Amazon and the internet, and why this is finally the chance to ultimately change your life for the better.

So for those of you who don't know, Amazon started out as an online book store back in 1994 before they became the online retail giant that we all know today. The scale of their operation has grown to unbelievable heights where it's even posed serious threats amongst all brick and mortar stores across the United States.

Having observed the early shift in consumer trend and behaviour, Jeff Bezos went on to become the richest man in the world by revolving his business around providing high-quality and affordable products delivered at incredible speeds. And that is exactly how Amazon was able to immensely capture the hearts of most consumers worldwide.

You are probably wondering by now, "Can I really make money with this business model?" To tell you honestly, it really isn't as hard as you might think. In a nutshell, Amazon FBA is basically a physical products business where you find an existing product on demand, slap your brand on the product and get a supplier to manufacture the products for you. You then ship it to an Amazon warehouse using a freight services, launch it to the 1st page, and you start making money as soon as a customer purchases your product on Amazon.

Plus the best part is, you won't ever need to pick & pack the products on your own as Amazon has got all the fulfillment process very well taken care of. With millions and millions of shoppers visiting the platform each day, these people already have their wallets open and they are ready to buy stuff. So your job is to simply create products that your customers will love and continue to buy for years and years to come.

So now, it's time for you to get excited because we're about to get into the meat of this book.

47 Powerful Secrets of a
7 Figure Amazon Seller

TIP #1: Focus on building a brand, rather than going for random product opportunities.

Most of the so-called "gurus" in the Amazon FBA space preach going for hot and random product opportunities, but this is not something I recommend you do. Instead, what I strongly preach is for you to choose a category, and focus on only launching products within that specific category.

See, brand building, especially in 2018 and beyond, is the name of the game and there are a lot of solid reasons why.

First off, building a brand in a specific category creates massive reputation for your brand name because as people in that market sees your product listings scattered everywhere, they start to associate your brand as being the best and most specialized for that specific category.

Another reason you want to build a brand is it allows you to scale quicker and more efficiently than you ever thought possible. See, once you build a brand name that people love and you own a massive list of people who raves about your products, it will be far way easier to scale & launch more and more new products into the Amazon marketplace. Why? Well first off, you've built a massive list which means that when launching, you don't need to giveaway as much units in order to rank on the 1st page. In fact, if you have a really successful list, you don't even need to do any giveaways and that alone can really save you a lot of money..

Lastly, building a brand gives you the opportunity to sell your Amazon FBA business for a massive payday. See, investors are not just looking for any Amazon FBA business, they want solid brands that serves a specific target market. So if you're going for random product opportunities, you're not building a sellable Amazon FBA business. But instead, if you focus on launching products within a single brand, you're looking at a huge opportunity to sell later on at a massive valuation.

What's even more amazing is, there are a lot of brands out there that started out on Amazon which are currently being valued at 7, 8 and even 9-figures. In fact, there's even one specific brand known as Anker which has already closed in on a billion dollar valuation. Mind-blowing, right? Exactly! That is why you want to focus on building a brand. I mean, that reason alone should be enough to convince you to focus on building a brand, instead of just going for random products.

TIP #2: Sell what the market is already buying.

It used to be that you needed an original idea in order to come up with a product and launch a real business, but not anymore!

See, in our world today and especially with Amazon FBA, you get to see and know exactly what products are hot and already selling on Amazon.

So instead of trying to come up with a smart new invention that you're not even sure there's a market for, just sell what people are already buying.

This is such a simple principle, but I promise you that it's one of the biggest keys to real success on Amazon FBA.

Now, there are two main ways to figure out if a product is already in demand on Amazon.

The first way is using the BSR. The BSR or best sellers rank is basically Amazon's way for calculating sales velocity per category. So a product with the #1 BSR in the toys & games category indicates that it's selling the most amount of units in that category. To put it simply, you want to sell products in markets full of listings with low BSR.

Now, another way is to use tools like Jungle Scout and Market Intelligence. These tools are Chrome extensions that you can use to extract data from each listing such as the estimated revenue per month, number of reviews, and a whole bunch of other stuff! Note that I said estimated, and not exact, as it is not possible to know exactly how many units a specific listing is selling every month.

Now, once you pull up these extensions on Amazon's search page, you'll see what is essentially a spreadsheet of all the important data. And if the numbers show you that the whole market is making good money, then that is a perfect sign that you should dive deeper into that product. Personally, I prefer launching products that could potentially make me around $5,000 - $20,000 every month, and you'll see why in a later tip.

The point here is, do not reinvent the wheel. This is not about what you're passionate about. We want to make money here so go sell what's already selling on Amazon and give the market what they want.

TIP #3: Don't go swimming into the deep Red Ocean.

So one of my favorite concepts in business is this thing called the Red Ocean and the Blue Ocean.

See, in the Red Ocean, businesses literally do whatever they can just so they could grab the biggest piece of the pie. And as the pie gets crowded and saturated by all this competition, products in that market starts becoming commodities and profits starts sailing away. Now, the reason why it's called Red Ocean is because the cut-throat competition between these massive companies turns the ocean bloody red.

Now, in the Blue ocean, competition is basically irrelevant. These are untapped markets where new companies can realistically go in and grab a big piece of the pie. This is where the profits are for you as a small business owner, and this is the ocean you want to be swimming in.

So, how do you take that concept and apply it to your Amazon FBA business?

It's simple, you want to only launch products in Blue Ocean markets. To make this concept even less confusing for you, imagine this for a second. The creatures that live in the Blue Ocean are these cute little clown fishes and angel fishes. On the other hand, big hungry sharks are lurking to kill anyone that tries to mess with their business. And that is exactly why you want to avoid Red Ocean markets.

Now, I hope that was a pretty interesting concept for you to hear but let's make that more actionable for you as a seller on Amazon

What Blue Ocean means on Amazon is product opportunities where competition is almost irrelevant. These are markets where poor quality listings are making tons of money even without having a lot of reviews. These types of opportunities allow you to go in and dominate a market on Amazon.

So you want to find Blue Ocean opportunities and only focus on launching products in those markets.

Master this tip right here, and you will become an unstoppable force in the Amazon FBA world.

TIP #4: Don't sell fad, seasonal, and trendy products.

Ideally, you wouldn't want to sell these types of products, especially if you're someone who's just getting started, and I'm so excited to share with you why. But before we get into that, let us first define the difference between these three so you could have a better understanding going forward.

These 3 things aren't really one and the same, but seasonal products only sell during certain times of the year. Take for example a product like winter jackets, obviously, the demand for winter jackets are going to be slower during the summertime, and sales are surely to gain traction whenever the winter seasons are around the corner.

Fad & trendy products, on the other hand, are products that sell like crazy for a short period of time and literally dies off to the abyss later on.

These products are not meant to be around forever as they have crazy demand simply because of the sudden increase in popularity.

The best example for this would be the fidget spinners. This product became one of the best-selling items on Amazon in early 2017, and this fad only lasted for around 4 to 5 months. This catastrophic event caused a lot of Amazon sellers to lose their business, which led to mountain-piles of fidget spinners collecting dust in the warehouse.

Now that you're aware about these types of products, let us talk about the benefits in hindsight, of implementing this specific tip.

One of the biggest decisions that you have to make in your business is deciding the amount of units to order, as well as when to order your inventory. See, selling seasonal, fad, or trendy products will surely give you lots of headache in terms of forecasting your inventory and managing your business as a whole.

Long story short, just don't ever sell one of these to make your life easier. You'll thank me later.

So 2 quick and easy ways to know whether a product is seasonal, trendy, or a fad is to use awesome tools such as Keepa and Google Trends.

Now, let's first talk about Keepa. This one is super easy to use, just find it on Google and download the Chrome extension. This tool is amazing because it loads up an easy-to-use graph on a product page, and it allows you to see historical data of a specific listing. This means that you can see if the BSR of a product is low during certain times of the year, as well as if it's really high during specific months. If products in a market consistently shows low BSR throughout the year, then that is a good sign that you're not launching a seasonal product. On the other hand, if a market has only existed for less than 6 months, I'd totally stay away from that, as you could be looking at a fad or a trendy item.

Let's move over to Google Trends. This is a great tool because you can type in a search term on Google Trends, and you'll instantly see a graph showing the search volume range for that specific search term during certain times of the year. Perhaps the best part about Google Trends is that you can get search data from 5 or even 10 years ago, and this allows you to see a clearer picture of the trend.

So avoid this costly mistake and use these 2 tools to save yourself from investing thousands of dollars into dead inventory.

TIP #5: Profits are the lifeblood of your business.

Just like in any physical products business, profit margins are everything. Because if you don't make money, you basically don't have a business.

So if you really want to start making money on Amazon, you definitely need to understand the importance of making sure that the product you're looking at is really something worth pursuing.

Because the last thing that you want is to spend days or weeks trying to get a product up and running, only to find out that the product you're trying to launch is not even profitable to begin with.

So personally, I'd like to see a healthy 30% profit margin as this gives you a margin for error.

To calculate your product's potential profit, you can use the FBA revenue calculator to get a rough estimation on your numbers. And note that I said estimation, because you would never really get to know your exact true numbers until you get a full price quote from your supplier.

So definitely always look at your potential profit margins before moving forward, as this will not only help you make better business decisions, it can also help you avoid launching products with tight and compressed profit margins.

TIP #6: Watch out for patented products.

Save yourself! And don't ever attempt to sell products with a patent, especially if you want to avoid any legal issues in the future.

See, some of the products that you'll encounter on Amazon will be protected by a patent, and selling such products could get you in deep deep trouble.

So, what exactly is a patent? Well, I'd first like to explain that there's 2 types of patents. The first one is called a utility patent, this protects a product's mechanics and functions. The second one is what we call a design patent, this type of patent protects the design and look of a product.

Now, how do you know if the product you found is patented?

The best way to do a patent search is to simply Google search the name of your product and include the word 'patent' in the end. You'll then see some results from Google patents, and a couple other sites. Start to scan through the data with either Google patents or USPTO to confirm the patent. If any of the written text clearly describes anything about how your product functions or looks, that could be the patent we're talking about.

Now, I'm not an attorney so this is not meant to be legal advice, but in cases that you are not certain about the product you found, make sure to get yourself a patent attorney and let them analyze the patent for you so that you are not leaving anything to chances.

TIP #7: Products that are priced $15 - $60 is the perfect price range.

You're probably wondering, "is there such a thing as a perfect price range?"

I think you'll be amazed to find out that there actually is. See, going after products within the $15 to $60 price range means that you're taking advantage of the impulse buying psychology of these consumers.

So as an Amazon seller, keep in mind that we want to attack the subconscious brain because this part of the brain is what drives the impulse buying behaviour of these consumers. This also means that they'll buy without thinking too hard about it. And they don't even have to seek with their spouses or parents before making a purchase, which makes buying products in the $15 - $60 price range a breeze.

And so anything beyond the $60 price range, their guards are up. And they'll most likely have to do more research to make sure they're making the right decision, which makes purchasing items above $60 way harder.

On the other hand, it will be very hard to make a profit selling products below $15, and that is why I suggest you find products above the $15 mark.

So definitely consider using this tactic. Also understand that I'm not saying people won't ever buy products beyond this price range, because they do. But the $15 to the $60 price range has been proven time and time again to trigger the impulse buying psychology of these consumers, and it can really blow up your sales as a seller on Amazon.

Now, if you're enjoying this audiobook so far, I would appreciate it if you could just take a minute of your time to leave a short review on Audible.com.

TIP #8: Be on the lookout for decreasing price trends.

Imagine finding a crazy profitable product and as you're getting all excited and ready to launch, the prices on page 1 suddenly drops drastically. Now, this is one of the worse things that could ever happen to you as an Amazon seller because at this point, I'm afraid that you're too late to back out.

So how do you prevent this from ever happening to you?

The absolute best way is to download the Keepa price tracker and simply check the historical unit price of your competitors' products.

Now, while it's normal for an Amazon listing to decrease prices from time to time, you wouldn't want to see it consistently drop for 6 months straight. Because continuous decrease in prices are clear signs that a product is about to crash and burn, and this is going to slowly drain your profit margins until you're literally left with nothing in your pockets.

So once you see a product with a decreasing price trend, stay away from that product immediately and do not fall into the trap of the price war.

TIP #9: Don't go into keywords where there are lots of big and reputable brands.

Nike, Adidas, Apple, do any of these brand names sound familiar to you? I bet!

This tip serves as a warning that if you see any big and reputable brands in a market, you should immediately avoid it.

Why? Because they have a solid competitive advantage as these brands own massive lists of buyers, plus they have loyal customers that spread word-of-mouth about their products.

Another thing is, whenever people type in a search term on Amazon's website and they see these big brand names. Who do you think they'll choose? Your private label brand or the popular brand who's been around for decades building massive reputation? Exactly!

It's just not a good idea. I mean, I've been selling on Amazon for over 3 years and I still don't launch these type of products, so just don't!

TIP #10: Never ever get married to a product.

I know exactly how it feels to find a crazy lucrative product. You get butterflies in your stomach, and you're like a kid again, all excited about the future!

Until bam! The numbers drop and the future suddenly doesn't look as bright anymore. Do you still launch the product or do you start researching new product opportunities all over again?

See, most people would still launch their product despite of the numbers getting ugly because they don't understand the fundamental mindset of product selection which is, never ever get married to a product.

Because the truth is, the numbers don't lie. And if the data is clearly telling you that a product is no longer profitable, set your emotions aside and start looking for the next profitable product opportunity right now.

TIP #11: Avoid electronics, breakable products, and items with a lot of moving parts.

These 3 types of products are what I like to call headache products.

Why? Because they give you a ton of problems, and customers will be much more likely to complain about defects, broken units, and missing parts, therefore leaving negative reviews on your listing.

These are the products that you'll regret doing later on simply because it brings a lot of stress to you as an Amazon seller, and it also increases your chance of having a failed product.

Just try thinking about it. Electronic products have lots of complex parts that goes with it, and it's just much more likely to have defects rather than a simpler product like chalkboard.

Breakable products on the other hand, as the name suggests, they break easily. These are products like whiskey glass, mason jars, and dining plates so stay away from those.

Now, let's talk about products with a lot of moving parts. The biggest problem with these is the product arriving to a customer with missing or broken parts.

Just trust me on this one. You want to avoid these 3 types of products at all costs, especially if you're a new seller on Amazon.

But I want to include a pro tip here. See, you can definitely think outside the box and come up with ways for getting away with the issues that comes with selling these types of products. Because there are definitely sellers out there successfully selling these products so it's not like it's impossible. I'm just writing this tip to serve as a warning sign for new Amazon sellers.

TIP #12: Use Amazon's search bar to find profitable product opportunities.

This is definitely one of my favorite ways to find profitable markets because you are basically taking advantage of Amazon's search database.

See, Amazon's search bar has an auto-suggestion feature which gives suggestions of what customers are already searching for on Amazon.

So I have discovered 2 ways for best using Amazon's auto-suggest feature. The 1st is what I like to call the QWERTY method, as in the classic QWERTY keyboard. What you want to do here is start typing in random letters like "T-R-A" into Amazon's search bar, and as Amazon starts auto-suggesting a bunch of keywords, your job is to look further into those search terms and see whether it's a potential product for you to sell.

The 2nd way is what I like to call the market method. This one focuses on typing markets into Amazon's search bar. Take for example the word, "dog". As you search for the word "dog" on Amazon, it will start auto-suggesting keywords that also contains the word dog in it like dog leash. Now, all of sudden, you just found a ton of product opportunities to potentially launch in the dog market. And that is why the market method is so powerful!

Looking at a 10,000 foot overview, these methods are all about taking advantage of Amazon's advanced search database, as well as brainstorming different markets and letters so that you could find more potential product opportunities to launch on Amazon.

TIP #13: Build a private label empire around singles, and not home runs.

I'd first like to share a short story with you that relates so perfectly to this tip.

See, before having massive success on Amazon, I had one big product failure.

Guess why that product failed? It was because I got greedy and went after a home run product with crazy demand.

See, having the "home run" mindset will surely set you up for failure everytime, and this is why you should pay close attention.

There's a lot of reasons you should build your private label empire around singles and not home runs. 1 of the biggest reasons is if one product dies, then you still have 5 other products making you money. Your whole income being dependent on 1 home run product just isn't the safest way to play this private label game. So take Warren Buffett's advice, and don't put all your eggs into one basket.

Another reason you want to go after singles, is because homerun products attract hijackers like a magnet. And if you've ever sold on Amazon before, you know that hijackers are a pain in the ass to deal with.

You're also much more likely to strike out and launch products that fails when you're going after homerun products. Just like in my favorite sport, baseball, the batters who try to go after the most homeruns are usually the ones who strike out the most.

Lastly, a homerun product requires massive investments for ordering the inventory, launching it, and keeping it in stock. This puts your capital at risk, especially when considering the fact that your listing will be attracting a ton of hijackers.

Bottom line is, do not sell homerun products. Instead, look for singles and product opportunities with the potential to make $5,000 to $20,000 in revenue every month.

TIP #14: Always make sure your product is differentiated.

This is one of the biggest mistakes I see new sellers make on Amazon. See, a product that isn't differentiated is basically a commodity. Some sellers might say that their low prices is what makes their products stand out but trust me on this one, you never want price to be your sole differentiator because it's going to cut your profits down to zero and even negative.

Also think about this. If you have a product successfully selling on Amazon and suddenly, a new seller shows up and launches a massively differentiated product. That seller is going to steal a ton of your profits away just because of the simple fact that he or she really went the extra mile to create the best product in the market.

So ask yourself, "why would someone choose your product over your competitors'?" Once you really have a solid and clear answer to that question, then you're definitely on the right track.

So remember, always make sure your product is differentiated.

TIP #15: Leverage Amazon customer reviews to create an amazing product.

This is hands down the best way to create an amazing product.

You'd be shocked to see just how many things people are complaining about in these review sections, especially in the 2, 3 and 4 star reviews. It is just insane, and it also presents a wonderful opportunity for you to go in and solve these customer's pain points.

By the way, the reason that I don't include 1 star in there is because most of these reviews are usually very negative, and don't give constructive criticism. Some are even left by blackhat competitors.

So make sure to always analyze your competitor's reviews to see how you can create a product that totally blows your competition out of the water.

TIP #16: Bundle products together to add value and increase sales.

Let me ask you something. Given that the prices aren't too far from each other, would you rather purchase a chopping board on its own or this chopping board that goes with an awesome stainless steel kitchen knife.

I think we can both agree that the knife and chopping board bundle appeals way better to someone who's looking for chopping boards, right?

It would just entice the people that are shopping because the knife is such a perfect complementary add-on item to the chopping board.

So bundling is really one of the best ways you could differentiate your product and make a ton of sales.

Now, let's get into the meat and potatoes of how to bundle your product.

2 of my favorite ways to find complementary products to bundle with your primary item is using the "Frequently Bought Together" and "Customers Who Also Bought" section.

So midway through the product page of every listing on Amazon, there will be 2 sections called "Frequently Bought Together" and "Customers Who Also Bought". These 2 sections basically show you what specific products are being frequently bought together with the primary item. By leveraging this data, you can now go on to create a bundle that truly stands out in the marketplace.

Another way to find awesome add-on products is just brainstorming on top of your head. Just ask yourself, what item can I add to the main product that will get customers to rave about it? Just by asking that question, you should be able to come up with some interesting bundle ideas.

Now, there's 2 things to keep in mind when bundling.

First off, you'd usually want to bundle small add-on items. This means items that cost only an extra dollar or 2 to manufacture wherein the product package doesn't get too big to the point where it starts jacking up your shipping rates, storage fees, and fulfillment fees.

Second is the bundle needs to make sense because if it doesn't, then it just won't work, simple as that!

This truly is one of the most amazing ways to differentiate so definitely consider this for your next products.

TIP #17: Design an amazing product packaging that increases perceived value.

This is a great way to differentiate and it's truly unfortunate that a lot of sellers are still not taking advantage of this.

See, I used to be like most sellers. I would not pay to get an awesome packaging design done and they just looked ugly. But I've since learned from those mistakes and now, I always make sure to have the best designers working on my packaging designs.

Why? Because it's totally worth it! An amazingly designed product packaging can massively increase your product's perceived value and in turn, boost your conversions.

It will also make your product stand out, especially in a market where the competitors have terrible packaging design.

As for where to get an amazing packaging design, 2 of my favorite places are OutlineMatic and 99Designs.

So with this, make sure to always get an amazing packaging design done for all of your products!

TIP #18: Quantity changes to make your product stand out.

One of the most foolproof methods to stand out in a sea of competition is to market products in different quantity packs.

So if I'm looking to launch a product like tissue rolls, why not just increase the quantity and market a pack of 24. Now, that would appeal to consumers a lot stronger simply because they'll feel that this product has way more value to offer.

Now, a rule of thumb for quantity packs is it has to make sense not only to you, but also to your target market as well. Because remember that this product is not for you, it's for your target market so it definitely has to make sense to them or else, they won't buy it.

So take note of this and definitely consider marketing your next product as a quantity pack.

TIP #19: Change color and size to appeal to people's different needs in a market.

Would you agree that certain people prefer different colors and sizes? You probably would, right? I mean, you might like the color blue but not everybody else does. Some people just loves the color red or maybe orange. And the same thing applies to sizing as well.

This is such a great way to differentiate your products on Amazon. Just imagine this, if you're in a market where everybody is selling black fireproof bags and you come in with a blue one, you're going to appeal to everybody that likes the color blue. And since you're the only seller with a blue fireproof bag, you're literally getting all the sales from shoppers who prefer the color blue.

Now, my favorite way for knowing what color or size will most likely appeal to consumers is using an awesome service called PickFU.

PickFu is amazing because you can pay them to get people to answer your poll. What you can do is ask consumers if they would prefer your product in blue, red, black, or white. And if most answered blue, then it's obvious what you should be going for.

So go ahead and look into color and size changes for differentiating your next product on Amazon!

TIP #20: Launch multiple listings in a single product opportunity.

This is my best-kept secret for completely dominating less competitive markets, and I'm very excited to share this with you! See, launching multiple listings in less competitive product opportunities has proven that you can really dominate a market and make boatloads of money with a single product opportunity.

Now, the key here is you want to only use this strategy for markets with low competition, and that is really important because we want to grab the biggest piece of the pie.

So for you to easily grasp this strategy, I want you to start looking at Amazon listings like real estate. Each listing on Amazon is a real estate and the closer they are to the top of the 1st page, the more valuable the property is. So what you want to do is flood the 1st page with as many listings as possible. By doing that, consumers are going to start perceiving your brand as the no. 1 seller for that specific product.

Now, let's talk about how you can implement this strategy into your business!

First off, you'll need a low competition product opportunity for this strategy to really work because this just won't be as effective in more competitive markets, as there is another specific strategy we'll be talking about in a later tip for crushing it in more competitive markets.

But essentially, what you want to do is launch multiple unique listings in a low competition product opportunity. And by unique, I mean each listing you launch needs to have its own differentiating factor. So with that, you can launch items with different bundles, quantity packs, colors, and sizes. Honestly, there's really no limit to the ways you can differentiate and that's what makes this even more exciting!

If you're not convinced yet, here are some more amazing things I realized through implementing this strategy.

First is you are going to have a smoother supply chain, and stronger negotiating power. Why? Because instead of going from one random product to the next, you will be focused on launching a single product. This means you are going to be ordering from the same supplier over and over again which is going to build credibility and trust between your companies. This presents an awesome opportunity to absolutely sweeten up your deals.

Another amazing thing is you are creating a high barrier to entry for that market. See, as you launch more and more listings in a market, it will be very daunting for new sellers to come in and try to steal away your profits.

If that doesn't convince you how great of a strategy this is, I don't know what will!

So definitely go all in on this powerful secret!

Now, if you're enjoying this audiobook so far, I would appreciate it if you could just take a minute of your time to leave a short review on Audible.com.

TIP 21: Launch a ton of variations under one listing to compete in more competitive markets.

From my years of selling on Amazon, the best strategy I've found for competing in more competitive markets is to launch a lot of variations under one listing.

See, there are listings in competitive markets that owns majority of the market share. So you launching a brand new product into that market and dominating is totally unrealistic.

What's realistic though is for you to still generate a solid amount of profits, and that's what launching a ton of variations under one listing can do for you.

So basically, what's happening here is we are combining the sales of all these different variations to boost the rankings of only 1 listing. And in more competitive markets, you are definitely going to need tons and tons of sales in order to rank and stick on the 1st page. Now, that is what makes launching different variations under one listing such a powerful method.

A pro tip for easily coming up with ideas for all these different variations is to use all the differentiation tactics we've talked about in this book.

So with this powerful strategy in your arsenal, you will definitely have what it takes to compete in more competitive markets!

TIP #22: Create amazing photos to massively increase your conversions.

From my years of selling on Amazon, it is indeed true when they say that a picture is worth a thousand words.

See, spending as much as $1,000 for high-quality images has been proven to massively increase conversions and sales. In fact, this is perhaps one of my biggest secrets as an Amazon seller and that is I am willing to pay a lot of money for awesome crisp-quality pictures.

Most sellers though try to cut corners and save money on their photos, but trust me, this is not something you want to cheap out on as poor quality images can really mean the difference between a listing that sells like crazy and a listing that doesn't even sell a single unit.

So here are some general guidelines for awesome listing images.

First off, you want at least 2 white background photos that clearly features your product in different angles. Now, this is a must whether you like it or not because Amazon requires a white background photo for your main hero image. Another pro tip is you can have 3d rendering done for your white background photos to make it look extra clean and crisp.

Next is, you want at least 3 lifestyle images showing the product being used by the target demographic. This is super powerful as lifestyle images really allow the consumers to visualize themselves using the product.

And last but certainly not the least is having an amazing infographic that clearly specifies the features and benefits of your product. Now, the goal of your infographic is very simple, that is to sell them on why your product is the one they need.

My 2 favorite go-to places for awesome photos are Viral Launch and Pixel Perfect Photography, so definitely check these guys out and make sure to get the best photos done for all of your products!

TIP #23: Write great copy in your listing's bullets and descriptions.

One of the biggest things that always makes my products stand out from the competition is that I apply sales copy into every single one of my product's bullets and descriptions.

Now, some people just prefer to pay someone to get their listing created but this is not something I recommend as I have yet to find a great copywriter out there that specializes in writing bullets & descriptions for Amazon listings.

So let's dive into the 3 ways I apply sales copy into my bullets and descriptions.

First off, sell people with benefits and not features. See, this is one of the most common mistakes sellers make when writing their bullets. They write a bunch of specs and features that customers don't even care about. But if you really want to increase your conversions, tell consumers about the benefit of your product and how it makes their life better and easier.

Next is, write in a way where consumers can imagine themselves using your product. A great way to do that is to use power words. Remember, people buy based on emotions so the reason these power words are so awesome is because they are basically words that attacks the subconscious brain and hits people emotionally. Here's a quick list of 15 power words you can use to write awesome bullets and descriptions: new, you, because, free, now, imagine, instant, love, guaranteed, spectacular, remarkable, sensational, amazing, breathtaking, and astonishing. Make sure to take notes of that in your notebook. Now, there are lots of other power words you can add to your arsenal, so just do a quick search on Google and you should find more.

The third thing is, you want to make sure that highly searched keywords are visible in your bullets and descriptions as this has proven to boost your rankings.

So just by implementing everything you learned in this tip, you should be able to write awesome bullets & descriptions.

TIP #24: Rank for long-tail keywords to get massive exposure on your listing.

This tip is definitely one you should be paying attention to, especially if you want to get massive exposure on your listing.

Now, for you to easily grasp this tip, you must first understand how keywords work. So, I want you to start looking at every product on Amazon as this giant tree. And as we all learned back in science class, a tree consists of one main trunk that leads up to other smaller branches. The same applies to every product you'll find on Amazon, as each product consists of one main keyword that leads to a lot of other smaller keywords, and these smaller keywords are what we call as long-tail keywords.

See, there's a ton of reasons why ranking for long-tail keywords is very crucial to your product's success. First off, these are the low hanging fruits of your keywords simply because it is less competitive. Going back to the tree example, the smaller branches AKA long-tail keywords, basically has less competition because it has less search volume. So this makes ranking for long-tail keywords much much easier.

Now to keep it clear, I am not saying that you shouldn't rank for the main keywords. I am simply saying that long-tail keywords are easier and less competitive to rank for and therefore, it's going to be smart for you to target these keywords, especially in the beginning.

Now, if you have thousands and thousands of dollars to invest on giveaways and ads, then that's a different thing as you could definitely start out your launch aggressively by targeting the biggest and most competitive keywords. But even me, being an Amazon seller for over 3 years, I still start out ranking for the long-tail keywords first before going out to rank for the main ones.

So definitely implement this game-changing tip to your next product launch!

TIP #25: Put the biggest and broadest keyword as the first words in your title.

This is a tip you must absolutely understand if you want to successfully sell on Amazon. See, in a listing, your title has the biggest impact on your keyword rankings. And the nearer a keyword is to the front of the title, the more priority Amazon gives to it for ranking. That's why it is super important to put your main and broadest keyword in the very front of your title.

Now, some sellers out there put their brand name first, but I highly recommend against that as nobody will probably ever search for your brand name on Amazon.

So once again, make sure to always put your biggest and broadest keyword in the very front of your title.

TIP #26: Don't price your products too low.

This is arguably one of the worse things you could do in your Amazon FBA business as pricing your products too low will not only leave you profit-less, but it will also decrease your conversions on a massive scale.

Now, understanding the difference between high pricing and cheap pricing is so crucial as it really affects how a consumer will ultimately perceive your product.

So by pricing your products too low, you are creating a perception in the consumer's mind that your product is cheap and something that's easily broken.

Pricing your products higher on the other hand gives consumers a more premium feel and they'll perceive your product as high quality.

While both approaches may work, I strongly recommend you price your products high because after all, we started this Amazon FBA business to make profits and selling cheaply-priced products on Amazon just won't cut it.

Now, as a general rule of thumb, you'd still want to competitively price your products against the selling price of your top competitors.

So, go ahead and take advantage of the wisdom in this tip!

TIP #27: Strive to provide the most top-notch quality products for your customers.

Many say that it's too late to start selling on Amazon, but that couldn't be further from the truth.

See, the truth is competition on Amazon has gotten fiercer year by year, but it doesn't mean that it's too late for you to sell on Amazon. It just means you have to play the cards you've been dealt with amazingly well.

Now, one thing I know for sure from my years of selling on Amazon is that doing the bare minimum of just sourcing a product and slapping it on Amazon doesn't work as well as it used to.

You have to truly put your heart and soul into creating the best products possible, especially if you want to make money, and I mean, who doesn't want to make money right? So there's just no other way to go about this private label game. Should you choose to sacrifice quality for lower prices or get lazy in this process, you are bound to fail before you even begin.

Now, this tip might sound obvious but I promise you that most sellers out there are still not focusing on on creating the best product for their customers and once you make this fundamental shift in your business, you will, without a shadow of a doubt, crush your competitors on Amazon FBA.

TIP #28: Focus on building a good relationship with your supplier.

Most sellers on Amazon are sleeping on an opportunity of a lifetime to build an amazing relationship with their suppliers, and because of that, they don't get to reap all the amazing benefits that comes along with having good relationships with a supplier.

Let me explain to you why building an amazing relationship with your supplier is key to running a successful Amazon business!

First off, you will have a smoother supply chain, as well as the ability to negotiate better terms. And these 2 things are very crucial when scaling your business.

But before you're able to build a good relationship with your supplier, I believe that it's critical for you to first understand what's going on inside their heads. So just imagine, and put yourself in your supplier's shoes. How would you want to be treated and talked to? How would you feel if a customer is being super pushy with the prices? Now, those are super interesting things to think about, as it will guarantee that you don't commit any rookie mistakes that ends up destroying your relationship!

Another pro tip is constant deposits are a must so talk to your suppliers regularly and not only when you're in need of something. Just share little things about your life and your business. Perhaps, you could even go as far as booking a plane ticket to China, and meeting them in person. But if you don't want to go that far, then that's totally fine. Just always remember to talk to them in a very friendly manner, and wish them well everytime you send a message.

Another solid tip is to create the perception that you're growing and scaling your business with them. This tip right here creates that shared vision and builds trust unlike anything.

So doing all those things will surely result in you building an awesome and lucrative relationship with your supplier that lasts for decades to come.

TIP #29 Make sure to work with a manufacturing company, and not a trading company.

You may be wondering why I'm strongly suggesting that you never work with a trading company, so allow me to convince you why.

Basically, a trading company acts as a middleman that outsources your products from a manufacturer, which means that you're technically handicapped here as there's a lot of negatives about not having direct access to your manufacturer.

See, everytime you're dealing with a trading company, you are most likely to receive jacked up prices as they have to make money in the process as well. And not only that, you also put yourself at a very high risk of having inconsistencies in the quality of your product, and this is definitely the last thing you want for a physical products business.

There's also the challenges of having to communicate with a trading company. It's just way more challenging to get your message across the board, not to mention that this also makes it harder for you to build a solid win-win relationship.

Another thing is, you run a small risk of delayed shipments as you virtually have no access to your manufacturer. Now, I'm not saying that all trading companies are like that, but I just want you to realize that you're the one who's at a lost here.

Working with a manufacturing company on the other hand, will provide you with direct access to your manufacturer and it's just less of a headache overall. You'll also notice that their prices are going to be significantly cheaper, simply because of the fact that there's no middleman, and you're directly working with the manufacturer of your product.

So I'm guessing that at this point, it's an obvious decision. But how do you know if you're working with a manufacturing company or a trading company?

The best method I've found is to simply look into the web product catalog of your supplier on Alibaba and see if they specialize in any specific type of product.

This is also what I like to call the Similar Thread Test. Let's say you're looking to sell a product like kitchen knives, of course you'd want your supplier to be focused on producing goods revolving around knives, or at least kitchen-related stuff. Because this gives you the confidence that they're much more likely to produce super sharp high-quality kitchen knives, which is exactly what you need in your business.

So definitely take action on this tip and make sure that you're working with a manufacturing company.

TIP #30: Use 1688 to negotiate better prices.

Negotiating better prices is the most obvious way to increase the profitability of your Amazon FBA business. But how do you even negotiate in the first place?

One of my best-kept secrets for negotiating better prices with my suppliers is using this website called 1688.com. This website is basically the Chinese version of Alibaba, and perhaps the greatest thing about it is that prices are way way cheaper compared to Alibaba.

So first off, what you want to do is translate your product name into the Chinese language using a tool like Google translate.

So if your product is a garlic press, simply translate "garlic press" into Chinese, and copy & paste the characters into the search bar on 1688.

Once you see the product, try to notice the different prices that are being offered by different manufacturers. For the most part, you'll see prices shown in Yuan which is China's official currency. So just make sure to always convert that into the US currency before going back with your supplier.

Now, if you've found that the prices on 1688 really is cheaper, then go ahead and feel free to tell that to your supplier. Because 9 times out of 10, they would lower the prices for you a little bit. But an important thing to keep in mind though is that it's not realistic for you to get the same prices on 1688 with your Alibaba supplier, as these prices are for local Chinese customers only, so don't even try to negotiate that hard with them or else, you might just end up destroying your relationship.

So go ahead and negotiate better prices with this awesome negotiation tactic!

Now, if you're enjoying this audiobook so far, I would appreciate it if you could just take a minute of your time to leave a short review on Audible.com.

TIP #31: Spy on your competitor's manufacturers to gain a competitive edge. (usaimportdata.com)

In every Amazon product opportunity you'll encounter, there's always going to be this one listing that just gets the most sales.

But did you know that you can actually spy on your top competitors and get to know exactly who their manufacturers are?

Now, while this method might not work all the time, I strongly believe that behind every best-selling piece on Amazon, is a manufacturer who has mastered the art, and that's the reason this technique is always worth a shot.

So the best resource to spy on your competitors is using a website called usaimportdata.com. Simply search for the brand name or the seller name of your top competitors, and as it goes through all the public information listed in the site, it's going to show you a ton of details that you could use to track the company name of your competitors' manufacturer. Now, I'm not going to get into the nitty-gritty of this, but with the information given in the site and your smarts, you should definitely be able to connect the dots.

TIP #32: Make sure to always get your inventory inspected.

Now, this is hands down the biggest mistake I made with my first product. See, I didn't pay a third-party inspection company to inspect the goods in China before it got shipped.

So basically, what happened is the product arrived to Amazon and it started selling a few units. Then a few day laters, the listing suddenly got hit with a ton of negative reviews. It was in that moment I realized that I messed up big time.

So long story short, you always want to make sure to get your inventory inspected by a credible third-party inspection company in China before you even consider shipping a single unit to the Amazon warehouse.

As for my most recommended third-party inspection company, it would definitely be AsiaInspection.

So let's now move on to the next tip!

TIP #33: Ask your supplier to protect your product ideas.

So imagine spending hours and hours trying to differentiate your product, only to find out that your supplier just sold your idea to a competitor, or even worse, they're selling it themselves!

You should never allow that to happen. See, the key is you want to build an understanding and create an agreement between you and your supplier that this product differentiation idea is exclusively yours, and therefore, they should not manufacture it for anyone else.

You should also explain to your manufacturers how it'll benefit them.

See, without your business, manufacturers basically don't have a business as your repeated orders are their lifeblood. So you have to make it clear that by making the product solely exclusive to you, you're going to have much more success as a seller on Amazon. And you having massive success on Amazon means they're going to have success together with you as your sole manufacturer.

So definitely implement this tip and protect your product ideas!

TIP #34: Be on the lookout for Chinese holidays.

One of the worst things that could ever happen to you as an Amazon seller is running out of inventory because all the time and effort you've spent to launch your product is just going to waste. Not to mention that you're also missing out on a ton of sales every single day that you're not in stock.

Now, sometimes your rankings might stick but this depends on how long you're out of stock for, as well as how strong your sales history is with Amazon.

To make the long story short, you'd never want to run out of inventory, ever.

And one of the things you can get hit with as a new Amazon seller is not knowing anything about the Chinese holidays and how it works. So during the Chinese holidays, understand that manufacturers are not open for business which means that you won't be able to place any orders and stock up on inventory.

So this is why you need to be prepared and stocked up before the month of February comes. Now, there are other holidays in China but the one I'm talking about here is the biggest holiday of all, also known as the Chinese New Year. So, I want you to understand that this is their most awaited time of the year, and it means a lot to them as this is when factory workers go back to catch up with their loved ones. So just understand that this is sacred for them.

And here's realistically what you should expect. Your manufacturer will most likely be on their holiday break for about 2 to sometimes even 4 weeks. So basically, you want to order an extra 2 to 4 weeks worth of inventory in preparation for the Chinese New Year.

This tip is massive so really make sure that you're always on the lookout for Chinese holidays.

TIP #35: Fix special payment terms to improve cash flow and scale your business.

If you want to scale efficiently and improve cash flow of your Amazon FBA business, then the way to do exactly that is to fix special payment terms with your supplier.

See, this is often overlooked by most sellers but trust me when I say that this is one of the most powerful tips I've ever received in my Amazon

FBA journey. Why? Because it's allowed me to scale my business in speeds I never even thought was possible!

So, how do you fix special payment terms? The 1st step is to build an amazing relationship with your supplier, as covered in tip #28. You can't just ask for special payment terms, you have to earn it, and you earn it by winning the trust of your supplier. Because if they don't trust you, you're not getting any special payment terms, simple as that.

So again, the 1st step is to build a solid relationship with your supplier.

Moving on to the next step: Once you've built an amazing relationship with your supplier to the point where you can really say that you've won their trust, it is now time for the big ask.

Don't get nervous here, just go ahead and tell them straight up that you want to fix a special payment term with them and make them realize that by giving you this, they are helping you scale your business way more efficiently, and remember that the scale of your private label business directly reflects the scale of their business as well.

Now, as for what kind of special payment terms to ask for, this will completely depend to you, as you also need to factor in how good of a relationship you have with your supplier.

To give you some context, the best payment term I've ever gotten from a supplier was paying 20% down payment, and having the rest of the 80% paid 2 months after the goods was finished. Now, just imagine how efficient my cash flow was after that agreement was made. I was getting paid by Amazon before I even needed to pay the balance with my supplier. Crazy, right?

So before you go out there and start asking for special payment terms, I want to give you a couple of reminders.

First is, some suppliers just don't give out special terms and there's really nothing you can do about it. At this point, you can just keep reordering from the same supplier especially if their products has been proven to deliver on quality.

Why not just find a new supplier? You may ask. The reason I don't suggest that is although fixing special terms is a solid hack that can allow you to scale quicker, it's not like this determines the success of your business. Plus, you don't want all your relationship building efforts to just go to waste.

Second reminder is, you don't want to be too pushy with your supplier as this can destroy the solid relationship that you've spent a lot of time building.

So with this in mind, the best way to go about this is to have that balancing act, or simply trusting your gut on what feels right for you.

TIP #36: Hire virtual assistants to automate and scale your business fast.

Regardless of whether you're scaling your Amazon FBA business, or you want to automate it so you can generate streams of cash on autopilot, this is the tip that you've been finally waiting for!

See, hiring virtual assistants are surely going to take your business to the next level. It doesn't matter if you're brand new or if you're an experienced seller. Leveraging the power of other people's time in your business is absolutely the smartest choice you could ever possibly make as it allows you to get way more done in less time.

Let's try to do the math here. Imagine having 5 or more people working on your business, and if each person worked 8 hours per day, you are getting at least 40 hours of hard work everyday without you even working for a single second!

Now, if you're someone looking to fully automate your private label business, I'll have to admit that it is totally possible, although that may depend to the extent of how far you want to automate it.

To help you understand what I mean, the more people you have working on your business, the more people that you'll need to handle as well, which also means that more money is being demanded from your payroll.

And unless that you've decided to even delegate the task of closely managing your team, you're just going to be filled with more responsibilities overall.

It's also a struggle to get the most productivity out of your team, because trust me, it can get real frustrating at times.

An interesting thing though is, while you're required to manage your people, you will soon realize that you're also taking loads of work off your shoulder.

Now, understand that you are the leader of your team so you'll have to spend time working on the things that matter the most, and as for the rest of the tasks that are redundant and boring, delegate it to your virtual assistant.

So go ahead and make your first hire, you can find awesome virtual assistants on OnlineJobs.ph.

TIP #37: Take advantage of the crazy demand in Q4.

Q4 is like heaven on Earth for Amazon sellers like you and me. Now, if you don't know what Q4 stands for, this is basically the 2 months leading up to the New Year. I wouldn't really consider October to be part of Q4 in terms of sales, as sales only really start ramping up in mid-November.

Now during Q4, there are tons of big holidays like Black Friday, Cyber Monday, and Christmas, and all these Q4 holidays will blow up your sales like the fireworks on New Year's Eve. I'm not exaggerating! Ok, maybe a bit. But you could really double your sales during this exciting period. In fact, it could even sometimes triple your sales. The amount of shoppers that are looking to buy products on Amazon during Q4 is just insane.

Here's another thing I believe you'll find very exciting, over 60 billion dollars was processed during Amazon's 2017 Q4!

This presents a massive opportunity for every Amazon seller and it's truly something you should be taking advantage of.

So how do you take advantage of the crazy demand in Q4?

First off, you should start testing higher price points. See, during Q4, especially starting mid-November, people are going to be buying a ton of gifts. They've got their mom, dad, sister, cousins, friends, and a whole bunch of other people they're going to buy gifts for.

This means that there's going to be a ton of impulsive buying decisions. And because of the nature of how consumers behave during these holidays, there's going to be a lot of opportunity for you to get quick sales at higher price points.

Also think about this. They're buying these gifts for their loved ones, and they would be more willing to spend more money just to get the highest quality product, as higher priced products does create the perception that a product is of higher quality.

So go ahead and test higher price points during Q4, but one thing to keep in mind is you want to slowly raise your price. You don't want to bump it up too fast and too quick. Instead, you want to increase it slowly in increments of a dollar per day.

Another way to take advantage of the crazy demand in Q4 is to setup lightning deals. But before we get into how awesome lightning deals are, I first want to note that you can only setup lightning deals if you have Brand Registry 2.0.

Now that we've got that out of the way, let's talk about the magic of lightning deals for Q4.

For those who don't know, lightning deals is basically offering your product at a 20 to 30 percent discount in one of the front pages of Amazon for a six-hour period.

A pro tip for lightning deals is to keep track of your time slot because you could end up running lightning deals that goes from midnight until 6 AM, and everybody's already sleeping so that's probably not the best time.

What will happen is Amazon will message you the time slot your lightning deal is going live at, so that you could cancel it if you see that it's setup to go live at a bad time.

Note that there's a fee for lightning deals, but I'd have to say that it's totally worth it!

Here's the last final tip on how you can take advantage of Q4. Amazon sales blow up during Q4, that means you're going to be selling a ton of units everyday.

So you need to have great inventory planning in place and make sure that you don't run out anytime during Q4 because if you do, you're going to miss out on a ton of delicious sales.

Now that you've got this tip dialed in, make sure to take action on it and prepare for the next upcoming Q4!

TIP #38: Think outside the box, and go against the grain.

Although I may have set some criterias of exactly what to look out for in a great product opportunity, that doesn't mean you can't think outside the box.

Of course, we want low competition and high demand products, that's a given. But all I'm giving you is an ultimate guide for making sure that your first few products on Amazon will make solid profits.

Now, remember when I said earlier that the $15 - $55 price range is where you want to be at, well that isn't super strict either. It's just a great guideline for you to follow especially when starting out on Amazon.

So definitely consider going against the grain and thinking outside the box once you've got a few products under your belt because by then, you are already more experienced, knowledgeable, and most importantly, you're already making money on Amazon.

TIP #39: Set up an LLC to provide yourself with liability protection.

Not setting up an LLC is a big mistake you're making, and that's why I had to make sure to include this tip here in this book.

See, running your business as a sole proprietorship holds you liable for everything and this could be your weak spot as an Amazon seller.

An LLC provides you with liability protection and also offers the benefit of recognizing the income from your business as being a pass-through onto your personal tax returns. This allows you to save on tax and makes it a lot easier.

An LLC also gives your business the legal structure to be able to scale. In short, an LLC is going to remove a lot of headaches that comes with scaling your business.

So regardless of whether you're a small or a large Amazon seller, I highly recommend you to go to LegalZoom and set up an LLC today.

A little disclaimer here, for anyone who has questions regarding setting up legal structures, I highly recommend you go consult with a corporate attorney.

TIP #40: Register a trademark to protect your brand and easily kick hi-jackers off your listing.

The main reason you want to register a trademark is because this is a requirement in order to register your brand in Brand Registry 2.0!

So what's this thing called Brand Registry, and how can this benefit your Amazon private label business? Well, there are tons of reasons why you should get started now. First off, having Brand Registry 2.0 gives you the ability to report counterfeiters through a report violation page.

Brand Registry also gives you the legal power to ask for identifiable information of the person trying to counterfeit your product. This allows you to use that information to be able to write up claims in your complaint so that you could threat them with a lawsuit. So this is definitely a solid way to protect your Amazon listing from hijackers.

Another benefit of Brand Registry, is that you will have special access to the enhanced brand content of Amazon where you're allowed to put images in the description part of your listing and it just makes your listing stand out so much more, which equates to you generating even more sales!

Also, don't forget that you're able to market your product in a more powerful way using Amazon Marketing Services.

So my final thoughts on this is I think that Brand Registry 2.0 could be Amazon's way of weeding out sellers who aren't serious about their business and rewarding those who are. After all, Amazon is a much better place for consumers when there are less counterfeit products floating around in the market.

A final reminder here is you want to register a trademark ASAP because they usually take 9 months to get approved. As for the service I use for registering a trademark, that would be LegalZoom.

So start the process of registering your brand in Brand Registry 2.0 today as it will definitely give you the edge over other sellers!

TIP #41: Know your accurate and true business numbers.

See, trying to run a business without understanding your numbers is like driving a car without a steering wheel.

I mean, it's good that you have a car and all but without the ability to steer left or right, you are bound to crash and burn.

The same applies in business. If you don't know your true and accurate business numbers, you won't have any solid data to work with and you'll be left playing the guessing game every time.

And playing the guessing game means that you'll be making poor business decisions and although your business might be doing well right now, it will eventually fall like the Roman Empire.

So make sure to have good accounting systems in place, and know your true business numbers. Now, as for my favorite & most recommended accounting software, it would definitely be Fetcher.

TIP #42: Save on shipping costs by consolidating your shipments.

Disclaimer: this is not applicable to new Amazon sellers as this tip is only for sellers that are already scaled and ordering tens of thousands of units.

Consolidating your shipments is putting all your shipments into one container so that you can cut your shipping costs and increase your profit margins. See, having multiple separate shipments is going to cost way more than consolidating all those shipments together into one container.

That's why this is one of the best-kept secrets for scaling an Amazon business because one thing you have to understand about scaling is it's all about efficiency and cash flow. And if you can cut your costs here and there, your business is really going to scale faster than you've ever imagined.

So once you really have what it takes to fill a 40 foot full container's worth of private label inventory, then go ahead and set up an FCL container with your freight forwarder.

TIP #43: Manage your inventory like a pro Amazon seller.

The most common thing I see happen to most new sellers is they either run out of stock or order way more inventory than needed.

That's why I want to give you the best advice on how to manage your inventory like a pro Amazon seller.

Let's say for example that a product is selling 10 units per day. Now, it usually takes 75 days from the day you drop your down payment to the day your product arrives on Amazon's warehouse.

So what I recommend you do is add the number 25 to 75. And now that you got the number 100, multiply that by the amount of units the product is selling per day. In this case, it's selling 10 units per day so you're going to be ordering a thousand units, which is a hundred days worth of inventory.

So once your inventory level drops to 750 units, that is a clear sign that you should quickly stock up on inventory as it will take another 75 days before your shipment arrives on Amazon!

One thing to keep in mind though is that your sales velocity will not always be consistent. So it's perfectly normal to have a few minor errors with your inventory planning. Just understand that, so that you don't beat yourself up when you make a mistake.

This is an advice I wish someone would have given to me when I first started selling on Amazon, and I just feel so pumped to be able to share this tip with you today!

TIP #44: Use a combination of Facebook Ads, Amazon PPC, and giveaways to launch and rank your product to the top of the 1st page.

Amazon loves outside traffic and if you pair that with PPC and giveaways in your launch, you're bound to reach the 1st page faster than ever.

It's like throwing a combination of punches. Facebook Ads is your jab, PPC is your hook, and then the giveaways is your uppercut. Now, that may be a strange analogy for this, but it's the perfect one.

See, when you're launching your product to the top of 1st page for keywords, there are other factors in play but perhaps the biggest factor is sales velocity. This means that you want a mix, and a combination of different tactics to increase sales velocity and further drive up your rankings.

And that is exactly what combining Facebook Ads, Amazon PPC, and giveaways does for you. It allows you to do an aggressive launch, wherein you're getting a mixture of massively discounted sales and full-price sales.

Amazon also loves it when you're driving outside traffic from places like Facebook or Instagram into their platform, and they'll reward you for it.

So for your next launch, I recommend you try out this trio of Facebook Ads, Amazon PPC, and giveaways.

I would have to note though that Facebook Ads is a lot trickier and you'd probably have to invest further to learn more in-depth stuff about that topic, which transitions perfectly into the next tip.

TIP #45: Become a continuous investor in yourself, and never stop adapting to the ever-evolving world of Amazon FBA.

Amazon FBA is an ever-evolving world which means that there will always be new changes to the Amazon marketplace, whether good or bad, and we will have to adapt to those changes quickly.

This is why this tip is very important. See, there were a lot of sellers in the past who had success but are not even making a dime on Amazon in today's time. Why? It's because of 2 simple reasons. 1st is, they stopped growing and investing in themselves. 2nd is, they didn't evolve and adapt to the new changes in the marketplace. Therefore, their businesses got swept away and died.

Remember this in your Amazon FBA business. Continuously invest in yourself so that you can keep on evolving & adapting to the ever-evolving changes in the marketplace.

TIP #46: Amazon FBA is a business, so treat it like one.

One of the biggest things that can stop you from achieving success with Amazon FBA is treating it like a side gig.

Look, this is not a side project or a lemonade stand. You're trying to build a massive private label empire here, which means that you're going to have to treat it like a real business.

So you definitely have to delay gratification and make sure to reinvest all the profits back into your business or else, your success won't last long. You also need to have good accounting in place to keep track of your business numbers. Another thing is you should absolutely be willing to invest money for the best quality services.

This tip is all about a massive mindset shift that is the foundation for most of the super successful Amazon sellers.

So once again, I just want to make sure you remember this one. Treat Amazon FBA like a business, and not like a side project.

TIP #47: Never ever give up, you are 3 feet away!

Although this might be the most cliche phrase ever, this is also one of the most powerful principles you could apply to your business and your life. And this is why I made sure to include this tip in this book.

Look, there are going to be tons of obstacles and roadblocks that will try to stop you from achieving success with Amazon FBA. Realize that all these struggles is just the universe testing you to see if you really do want it bad enough.

And here's one thing I know. Had I quit when I launched my first product that failed miserably, I would have never been able to create the lifestyle that I'm living today.

So whatever struggles you might be experiencing in your Amazon FBA journey, understand that it's a part of the process. And if you really want it bad enough, you should be able to push through those obstacles and never give up.

Another thing is you can never really say you've failed until you have quit. Because if you're still trying and launching products despite how many failures you've experienced, you are already a winner!

Now, one thing that changed my life is this very powerful mindset shift that I'm about to share with you right now.

I want you to start looking at all obstacles and adversities as a gift. Because once you make that simple mindset shift where you start looking at every obstacle as an advantage, you'll instantly start recognizing that everything in your life happens for you, instead of to you. So understand that you can't control the events that happen to you, but you can always control how you respond to those events. And that's what makes all the difference.

And lastly, never ever give up because you are three feet away from success!

Conclusion

Congratulations for getting to the end of this audiobook! Most people are not even willing to do that so your commitment just shows that you've got what it takes to succeed with Amazon FBA.

The 47 tips and secrets that you've learned in this short but powerful book took me years of trial and error to discover, and these really are my best-kept secrets for crushing it on Amazon FBA.

So take action and implement on what you think is best for your business because these are the tips that will surely take your game to the next level and help you build your own Amazon FBA empire that consistently generates passive income each and every month.

It truly has been a pleasure being able to share this information with you today. And I have indeed fulfilled my mission of spreading the word about Amazon and the rise of the internet, as well as why this is finally the chance to ultimately change your life for the better!

Now, if you believe this audiobook has provided you with tons of great value, then it would really mean the world to me if you could leave a short review on Audible. Thank you so much!

Printed in Great Britain
by Amazon